Password Organizer

Elite Journals

63 East 11400 South Suite #230
Sandy, UT 84070
EliteOnlinePublishing.com
EliteJournals.com

ISBN:

This Book Belongs To:

Date:

Table Of Contents

A	5
B	10
C	15
D	20
E	25
F	30
G	35
H	40
I	45
J	50
K	55
L	60
M	65
N	70
O	75
P	80
Q	85
R	90
S	95
T	100
U	105
V	110
W	115
X	120
Y	125
Z	130

A

PASSWORD ORGANIZER

WEBSITE:

USERNAME:

PASSWORD:

EMAIL USED:

SECURITY ANSWER:

NOTES:

WEBSITE:

USERNAME:

PASSWORD:

EMAIL USED:

SECURITY ANSWER:

NOTES:

WEBSITE:

USERNAME:

PASSWORD:

EMAIL USED:

SECURITY ANSWER:

NOTES:

WEBSITE:

USERNAME:

PASSWORD:

EMAIL USED:

SECURITY ANSWER:

NOTES:

PASSWORD ORGANIZER

WEBSITE:

USERNAME:

PASSWORD:

EMAIL USED:

SECURITY ANSWER:

NOTES:

WEBSITE:

USERNAME:

PASSWORD:

EMAIL USED:

SECURITY ANSWER:

NOTES:

WEBSITE:

USERNAME:

PASSWORD:

EMAIL USED:

SECURITY ANSWER:

NOTES:

WEBSITE:

USERNAME:

PASSWORD:

EMAIL USED:

SECURITY ANSWER:

NOTES:

PASSWORD ORGANIZER

WEBSITE:

USERNAME:

PASSWORD:

EMAIL USED:

SECURITY ANSWER:

NOTES:

WEBSITE:

USERNAME:

PASSWORD:

EMAIL USED:

SECURITY ANSWER:

NOTES:

WEBSITE:

USERNAME:

PASSWORD:

EMAIL USED:

SECURITY ANSWER:

NOTES:

WEBSITE:

USERNAME:

PASSWORD:

EMAIL USED:

SECURITY ANSWER:

NOTES:

PASSWORD ORGANIZER

WEBSITE:

USERNAME:

PASSWORD:

EMAIL USED:

SECURITY ANSWER:

NOTES:

WEBSITE:

USERNAME:

PASSWORD:

EMAIL USED:

SECURITY ANSWER:

NOTES:

WEBSITE:

USERNAME:

PASSWORD:

EMAIL USED:

SECURITY ANSWER:

NOTES:

WEBSITE:

USERNAME:

PASSWORD:

EMAIL USED:

SECURITY ANSWER:

NOTES:

B

PASSWORD ORGANIZER

WEBSITE:

USERNAME:

PASSWORD:

EMAIL USED:

SECURITY ANSWER:

NOTES:

WEBSITE:

USERNAME:

PASSWORD:

EMAIL USED:

SECURITY ANSWER:

NOTES:

WEBSITE:

USERNAME:

PASSWORD:

EMAIL USED:

SECURITY ANSWER:

NOTES:

WEBSITE:

USERNAME:

PASSWORD:

EMAIL USED:

SECURITY ANSWER:

NOTES:

PASSWORD ORGANIZER

WEBSITE:

USERNAME:

PASSWORD:

EMAIL USED:

SECURITY ANSWER:

NOTES:

WEBSITE:

USERNAME:

PASSWORD:

EMAIL USED:

SECURITY ANSWER:

NOTES:

WEBSITE:

USERNAME:

PASSWORD:

EMAIL USED:

SECURITY ANSWER:

NOTES:

WEBSITE:

USERNAME:

PASSWORD:

EMAIL USED:

SECURITY ANSWER:

NOTES:

PASSWORD ORGANIZER

WEBSITE:

USERNAME:

PASSWORD:

EMAIL USED:

SECURITY ANSWER:

NOTES:

WEBSITE:

USERNAME:

PASSWORD:

EMAIL USED:

SECURITY ANSWER:

NOTES:

WEBSITE:

USERNAME:

PASSWORD:

EMAIL USED:

SECURITY ANSWER:

NOTES:

WEBSITE:

USERNAME:

PASSWORD:

EMAIL USED:

SECURITY ANSWER:

NOTES:

PASSWORD ORGANIZER

WEBSITE:

USERNAME: ____________________

PASSWORD: ____________________

EMAIL USED: ____________________

SECURITY ANSWER: ____________________

NOTES: ____________________

WEBSITE:

USERNAME: ____________________

PASSWORD: ____________________

EMAIL USED: ____________________

SECURITY ANSWER: ____________________

NOTES: ____________________

WEBSITE:

USERNAME: ____________________

PASSWORD: ____________________

EMAIL USED: ____________________

SECURITY ANSWER: ____________________

NOTES: ____________________

WEBSITE:

USERNAME: ____________________

PASSWORD: ____________________

EMAIL USED: ____________________

SECURITY ANSWER: ____________________

NOTES: ____________________

C

PASSWORD ORGANIZER

WEBSITE:

USERNAME:

PASSWORD:

EMAIL USED:

SECURITY ANSWER:

NOTES:

WEBSITE:

USERNAME:

PASSWORD:

EMAIL USED:

SECURITY ANSWER:

NOTES:

WEBSITE:

USERNAME:

PASSWORD:

EMAIL USED:

SECURITY ANSWER:

NOTES:

WEBSITE:

USERNAME:

PASSWORD:

EMAIL USED:

SECURITY ANSWER:

NOTES:

PASSWORD ORGANIZER

WEBSITE:

USERNAME:

PASSWORD:

EMAIL USED:

SECURITY ANSWER:

NOTES:

WEBSITE:

USERNAME:

PASSWORD:

EMAIL USED:

SECURITY ANSWER:

NOTES:

WEBSITE:

USERNAME:

PASSWORD:

EMAIL USED:

SECURITY ANSWER:

NOTES:

WEBSITE:

USERNAME:

PASSWORD:

EMAIL USED:

SECURITY ANSWER:

NOTES:

PASSWORD ORGANIZER

WEBSITE:

USERNAME:

PASSWORD:

EMAIL USED:

SECURITY ANSWER:

NOTES:

WEBSITE:

USERNAME:

PASSWORD:

EMAIL USED:

SECURITY ANSWER:

NOTES:

WEBSITE:

USERNAME:

PASSWORD:

EMAIL USED:

SECURITY ANSWER:

NOTES:

WEBSITE:

USERNAME:

PASSWORD:

EMAIL USED:

SECURITY ANSWER:

NOTES:

PASSWORD ORGANIZER

WEBSITE:

USERNAME:

PASSWORD:

EMAIL USED:

SECURITY ANSWER:

NOTES:

WEBSITE:

USERNAME:

PASSWORD:

EMAIL USED:

SECURITY ANSWER:

NOTES:

WEBSITE:

USERNAME:

PASSWORD:

EMAIL USED:

SECURITY ANSWER:

NOTES:

WEBSITE:

USERNAME:

PASSWORD:

EMAIL USED:

SECURITY ANSWER:

NOTES:

D

PASSWORD ORGANIZER

WEBSITE:

USERNAME:

PASSWORD:

EMAIL USED:

SECURITY ANSWER:

NOTES:

WEBSITE:

USERNAME:

PASSWORD:

EMAIL USED:

SECURITY ANSWER:

NOTES:

WEBSITE:

USERNAME:

PASSWORD:

EMAIL USED:

SECURITY ANSWER:

NOTES:

WEBSITE:

USERNAME:

PASSWORD:

EMAIL USED:

SECURITY ANSWER:

NOTES:

PASSWORD ORGANIZER

WEBSITE:

USERNAME:

PASSWORD:

EMAIL USED:

SECURITY ANSWER:

NOTES:

WEBSITE:

USERNAME:

PASSWORD:

EMAIL USED:

SECURITY ANSWER:

NOTES:

WEBSITE:

USERNAME:

PASSWORD:

EMAIL USED:

SECURITY ANSWER:

NOTES:

WEBSITE:

USERNAME:

PASSWORD:

EMAIL USED:

SECURITY ANSWER:

NOTES:

PASSWORD ORGANIZER

WEBSITE:

USERNAME:

PASSWORD:

EMAIL USED:

SECURITY ANSWER:

NOTES:

WEBSITE:

USERNAME:

PASSWORD:

EMAIL USED:

SECURITY ANSWER:

NOTES:

WEBSITE:

USERNAME:

PASSWORD:

EMAIL USED:

SECURITY ANSWER:

NOTES:

WEBSITE:

USERNAME:

PASSWORD:

EMAIL USED:

SECURITY ANSWER:

NOTES:

PASSWORD ORGANIZER

WEBSITE:

USERNAME:

PASSWORD:

EMAIL USED:

SECURITY ANSWER:

NOTES:

WEBSITE:

USERNAME:

PASSWORD:

EMAIL USED:

SECURITY ANSWER:

NOTES:

WEBSITE:

USERNAME:

PASSWORD:

EMAIL USED:

SECURITY ANSWER:

NOTES:

WEBSITE:

USERNAME:

PASSWORD:

EMAIL USED:

SECURITY ANSWER:

NOTES:

E

PASSWORD ORGANIZER

WEBSITE:

USERNAME:

PASSWORD:

EMAIL USED:

SECURITY ANSWER:

NOTES:

WEBSITE:

USERNAME:

PASSWORD:

EMAIL USED:

SECURITY ANSWER:

NOTES:

WEBSITE:

USERNAME:

PASSWORD:

EMAIL USED:

SECURITY ANSWER:

NOTES:

WEBSITE:

USERNAME:

PASSWORD:

EMAIL USED:

SECURITY ANSWER:

NOTES:

PASSWORD ORGANIZER

WEBSITE:

USERNAME:

PASSWORD:

EMAIL USED:

SECURITY ANSWER:

NOTES:

WEBSITE:

USERNAME:

PASSWORD:

EMAIL USED:

SECURITY ANSWER:

NOTES:

WEBSITE:

USERNAME:

PASSWORD:

EMAIL USED:

SECURITY ANSWER:

NOTES:

WEBSITE:

USERNAME:

PASSWORD:

EMAIL USED:

SECURITY ANSWER:

NOTES:

PASSWORD ORGANIZER

WEBSITE:

USERNAME:

PASSWORD:

EMAIL USED:

SECURITY ANSWER:

NOTES:

WEBSITE:

USERNAME:

PASSWORD:

EMAIL USED:

SECURITY ANSWER:

NOTES:

WEBSITE:

USERNAME:

PASSWORD:

EMAIL USED:

SECURITY ANSWER:

NOTES:

WEBSITE:

USERNAME:

PASSWORD:

EMAIL USED:

SECURITY ANSWER:

NOTES:

PASSWORD ORGANIZER

WEBSITE:

USERNAME:

PASSWORD:

EMAIL USED:

SECURITY ANSWER:

NOTES:

WEBSITE:

USERNAME:

PASSWORD:

EMAIL USED:

SECURITY ANSWER:

NOTES:

WEBSITE:

USERNAME:

PASSWORD:

EMAIL USED:

SECURITY ANSWER:

NOTES:

WEBSITE:

USERNAME:

PASSWORD:

EMAIL USED:

SECURITY ANSWER:

NOTES:

F

PASSWORD ORGANIZER

WEBSITE:

USERNAME:

PASSWORD:

EMAIL USED:

SECURITY ANSWER:

NOTES:

WEBSITE:

USERNAME:

PASSWORD:

EMAIL USED:

SECURITY ANSWER:

NOTES:

WEBSITE:

USERNAME:

PASSWORD:

EMAIL USED:

SECURITY ANSWER:

NOTES:

WEBSITE:

USERNAME:

PASSWORD:

EMAIL USED:

SECURITY ANSWER:

NOTES:

PASSWORD ORGANIZER

WEBSITE:

USERNAME:

PASSWORD:

EMAIL USED:

SECURITY ANSWER:

NOTES:

WEBSITE:

USERNAME:

PASSWORD:

EMAIL USED:

SECURITY ANSWER:

NOTES:

WEBSITE:

USERNAME:

PASSWORD:

EMAIL USED:

SECURITY ANSWER:

NOTES:

WEBSITE:

USERNAME:

PASSWORD:

EMAIL USED:

SECURITY ANSWER:

NOTES:

PASSWORD ORGANIZER

WEBSITE:

USERNAME:

PASSWORD:

EMAIL USED:

SECURITY ANSWER:

NOTES:

WEBSITE:

USERNAME:

PASSWORD:

EMAIL USED:

SECURITY ANSWER:

NOTES:

WEBSITE:

USERNAME:

PASSWORD:

EMAIL USED:

SECURITY ANSWER:

NOTES:

WEBSITE:

USERNAME:

PASSWORD:

EMAIL USED:

SECURITY ANSWER:

NOTES:

PASSWORD ORGANIZER

WEBSITE:

USERNAME: ______

PASSWORD: ______

EMAIL USED: ______

SECURITY ANSWER: ______

NOTES: ______

WEBSITE:

USERNAME: ______

PASSWORD: ______

EMAIL USED: ______

SECURITY ANSWER: ______

NOTES: ______

WEBSITE:

USERNAME: ______

PASSWORD: ______

EMAIL USED: ______

SECURITY ANSWER: ______

NOTES: ______

WEBSITE:

USERNAME: ______

PASSWORD: ______

EMAIL USED: ______

SECURITY ANSWER: ______

NOTES: ______

G

PASSWORD ORGANIZER

WEBSITE:

USERNAME:

PASSWORD:

EMAIL USED:

SECURITY ANSWER:

NOTES:

WEBSITE:

USERNAME:

PASSWORD:

EMAIL USED:

SECURITY ANSWER:

NOTES:

WEBSITE:

USERNAME:

PASSWORD:

EMAIL USED:

SECURITY ANSWER:

NOTES:

WEBSITE:

USERNAME:

PASSWORD:

EMAIL USED:

SECURITY ANSWER:

NOTES:

PASSWORD ORGANIZER

WEBSITE:

USERNAME:

PASSWORD:

EMAIL USED:

SECURITY ANSWER:

NOTES:

WEBSITE:

USERNAME:

PASSWORD:

EMAIL USED:

SECURITY ANSWER:

NOTES:

WEBSITE:

USERNAME:

PASSWORD:

EMAIL USED:

SECURITY ANSWER:

NOTES:

WEBSITE:

USERNAME:

PASSWORD:

EMAIL USED:

SECURITY ANSWER:

NOTES:

PASSWORD ORGANIZER

WEBSITE:

USERNAME:

PASSWORD:

EMAIL USED:

SECURITY ANSWER:

NOTES:

WEBSITE:

USERNAME:

PASSWORD:

EMAIL USED:

SECURITY ANSWER:

NOTES:

WEBSITE:

USERNAME:

PASSWORD:

EMAIL USED:

SECURITY ANSWER:

NOTES:

WEBSITE:

USERNAME:

PASSWORD:

EMAIL USED:

SECURITY ANSWER:

NOTES:

PASSWORD ORGANIZER

WEBSITE:

USERNAME:

PASSWORD:

EMAIL USED:

SECURITY ANSWER:

NOTES:

WEBSITE:

USERNAME:

PASSWORD:

EMAIL USED:

SECURITY ANSWER:

NOTES:

WEBSITE:

USERNAME:

PASSWORD:

EMAIL USED:

SECURITY ANSWER:

NOTES:

WEBSITE:

USERNAME:

PASSWORD:

EMAIL USED:

SECURITY ANSWER:

NOTES:

H

PASSWORD ORGANIZER

WEBSITE:

USERNAME:

PASSWORD:

EMAIL USED:

SECURITY ANSWER:

NOTES:

WEBSITE:

USERNAME:

PASSWORD:

EMAIL USED:

SECURITY ANSWER:

NOTES:

WEBSITE:

USERNAME:

PASSWORD:

EMAIL USED:

SECURITY ANSWER:

NOTES:

WEBSITE:

USERNAME:

PASSWORD:

EMAIL USED:

SECURITY ANSWER:

NOTES:

PASSWORD ORGANIZER

WEBSITE:
USERNAME:
PASSWORD:
EMAIL USED:
SECURITY ANSWER:
NOTES:

WEBSITE:
USERNAME:
PASSWORD:
EMAIL USED:
SECURITY ANSWER:
NOTES:

WEBSITE:
USERNAME:
PASSWORD:
EMAIL USED:
SECURITY ANSWER:
NOTES:

WEBSITE:
USERNAME:
PASSWORD:
EMAIL USED:
SECURITY ANSWER:
NOTES:

PASSWORD ORGANIZER

WEBSITE:

USERNAME:

PASSWORD:

EMAIL USED:

SECURITY ANSWER:

NOTES:

WEBSITE:

USERNAME:

PASSWORD:

EMAIL USED:

SECURITY ANSWER:

NOTES:

WEBSITE:

USERNAME:

PASSWORD:

EMAIL USED:

SECURITY ANSWER:

NOTES:

WEBSITE:

USERNAME:

PASSWORD:

EMAIL USED:

SECURITY ANSWER:

NOTES:

PASSWORD ORGANIZER

WEBSITE:

USERNAME:

PASSWORD:

EMAIL USED:

SECURITY ANSWER:

NOTES:

WEBSITE:

USERNAME:

PASSWORD:

EMAIL USED:

SECURITY ANSWER:

NOTES:

WEBSITE:

USERNAME:

PASSWORD:

EMAIL USED:

SECURITY ANSWER:

NOTES:

WEBSITE:

USERNAME:

PASSWORD:

EMAIL USED:

SECURITY ANSWER:

NOTES:

PASSWORD ORGANIZER

WEBSITE:

USERNAME: __________

PASSWORD: __________

EMAIL USED: __________

SECURITY ANSWER: __________

NOTES: __________

WEBSITE:

USERNAME: __________

PASSWORD: __________

EMAIL USED: __________

SECURITY ANSWER: __________

NOTES: __________

WEBSITE:

USERNAME: __________

PASSWORD: __________

EMAIL USED: __________

SECURITY ANSWER: __________

NOTES: __________

WEBSITE:

USERNAME: __________

PASSWORD: __________

EMAIL USED: __________

SECURITY ANSWER: __________

NOTES: __________

PASSWORD ORGANIZER

WEBSITE:

USERNAME:

PASSWORD:

EMAIL USED:

SECURITY ANSWER:

NOTES:

WEBSITE:

USERNAME:

PASSWORD:

EMAIL USED:

SECURITY ANSWER:

NOTES:

WEBSITE:

USERNAME:

PASSWORD:

EMAIL USED:

SECURITY ANSWER:

NOTES:

WEBSITE:

USERNAME:

PASSWORD:

EMAIL USED:

SECURITY ANSWER:

NOTES:

PASSWORD ORGANIZER

WEBSITE:

USERNAME:

PASSWORD:

EMAIL USED:

SECURITY ANSWER:

NOTES:

WEBSITE:

USERNAME:

PASSWORD:

EMAIL USED:

SECURITY ANSWER:

NOTES:

WEBSITE:

USERNAME:

PASSWORD:

EMAIL USED:

SECURITY ANSWER:

NOTES:

WEBSITE:

USERNAME:

PASSWORD:

EMAIL USED:

SECURITY ANSWER:

NOTES:

PASSWORD ORGANIZER

WEBSITE:

USERNAME:

PASSWORD:

EMAIL USED:

SECURITY ANSWER:

NOTES:

WEBSITE:

USERNAME:

PASSWORD:

EMAIL USED:

SECURITY ANSWER:

NOTES:

WEBSITE:

USERNAME:

PASSWORD:

EMAIL USED:

SECURITY ANSWER:

NOTES:

WEBSITE:

USERNAME:

PASSWORD:

EMAIL USED:

SECURITY ANSWER:

NOTES:

J

PASSWORD ORGANIZER

WEBSITE:

USERNAME:

PASSWORD:

EMAIL USED:

SECURITY ANSWER:

NOTES:

WEBSITE:

USERNAME:

PASSWORD:

EMAIL USED:

SECURITY ANSWER:

NOTES:

WEBSITE:

USERNAME:

PASSWORD:

EMAIL USED:

SECURITY ANSWER:

NOTES:

WEBSITE:

USERNAME:

PASSWORD:

EMAIL USED:

SECURITY ANSWER:

NOTES:

PASSWORD ORGANIZER

WEBSITE:

USERNAME: ______________________

PASSWORD: ______________________

EMAIL USED: ______________________

SECURITY ANSWER: ______________________

NOTES: ______________________

WEBSITE:

USERNAME: ______________________

PASSWORD: ______________________

EMAIL USED: ______________________

SECURITY ANSWER: ______________________

NOTES: ______________________

WEBSITE:

USERNAME: ______________________

PASSWORD: ______________________

EMAIL USED: ______________________

SECURITY ANSWER: ______________________

NOTES: ______________________

WEBSITE:

USERNAME: ______________________

PASSWORD: ______________________

EMAIL USED: ______________________

SECURITY ANSWER: ______________________

NOTES: ______________________

PASSWORD ORGANIZER

WEBSITE:

USERNAME:

PASSWORD:

EMAIL USED:

SECURITY ANSWER:

NOTES:

WEBSITE:

USERNAME:

PASSWORD:

EMAIL USED:

SECURITY ANSWER:

NOTES:

WEBSITE:

USERNAME:

PASSWORD:

EMAIL USED:

SECURITY ANSWER:

NOTES:

WEBSITE:

USERNAME:

PASSWORD:

EMAIL USED:

SECURITY ANSWER:

NOTES:

PASSWORD ORGANIZER

WEBSITE:

USERNAME:

PASSWORD:

EMAIL USED:

SECURITY ANSWER:

NOTES:

WEBSITE:

USERNAME:

PASSWORD:

EMAIL USED:

SECURITY ANSWER:

NOTES:

WEBSITE:

USERNAME:

PASSWORD:

EMAIL USED:

SECURITY ANSWER:

NOTES:

WEBSITE:

USERNAME:

PASSWORD:

EMAIL USED:

SECURITY ANSWER:

NOTES:

K

PASSWORD ORGANIZER

WEBSITE:

USERNAME:

PASSWORD:

EMAIL USED:

SECURITY ANSWER:

NOTES:

WEBSITE:

USERNAME:

PASSWORD:

EMAIL USED:

SECURITY ANSWER:

NOTES:

WEBSITE:

USERNAME:

PASSWORD:

EMAIL USED:

SECURITY ANSWER:

NOTES:

WEBSITE:

USERNAME:

PASSWORD:

EMAIL USED:

SECURITY ANSWER:

NOTES:

PASSWORD ORGANIZER

WEBSITE:

USERNAME:

PASSWORD:

EMAIL USED:

SECURITY ANSWER:

NOTES:

WEBSITE:

USERNAME:

PASSWORD:

EMAIL USED:

SECURITY ANSWER:

NOTES:

WEBSITE:

USERNAME:

PASSWORD:

EMAIL USED:

SECURITY ANSWER:

NOTES:

WEBSITE:

USERNAME:

PASSWORD:

EMAIL USED:

SECURITY ANSWER:

NOTES:

PASSWORD ORGANIZER

WEBSITE:

USERNAME: ______

PASSWORD: ______

EMAIL USED: ______

SECURITY ANSWER: ______

NOTES: ______

WEBSITE:

USERNAME: ______

PASSWORD: ______

EMAIL USED: ______

SECURITY ANSWER: ______

NOTES: ______

WEBSITE:

USERNAME: ______

PASSWORD: ______

EMAIL USED: ______

SECURITY ANSWER: ______

NOTES: ______

WEBSITE:

USERNAME: ______

PASSWORD: ______

EMAIL USED: ______

SECURITY ANSWER: ______

NOTES: ______

PASSWORD ORGANIZER

WEBSITE:

USERNAME:

PASSWORD:

EMAIL USED:

SECURITY ANSWER:

NOTES:

WEBSITE:

USERNAME:

PASSWORD:

EMAIL USED:

SECURITY ANSWER:

NOTES:

WEBSITE:

USERNAME:

PASSWORD:

EMAIL USED:

SECURITY ANSWER:

NOTES:

WEBSITE:

USERNAME:

PASSWORD:

EMAIL USED:

SECURITY ANSWER:

NOTES:

L

PASSWORD ORGANIZER

WEBSITE:

USERNAME:

PASSWORD:

EMAIL USED:

SECURITY ANSWER:

NOTES:

WEBSITE:

USERNAME:

PASSWORD:

EMAIL USED:

SECURITY ANSWER:

NOTES:

WEBSITE:

USERNAME:

PASSWORD:

EMAIL USED:

SECURITY ANSWER:

NOTES:

WEBSITE:

USERNAME:

PASSWORD:

EMAIL USED:

SECURITY ANSWER:

NOTES:

PASSWORD ORGANIZER

WEBSITE:

USERNAME:

PASSWORD:

EMAIL USED:

SECURITY ANSWER:

NOTES:

WEBSITE:

USERNAME:

PASSWORD:

EMAIL USED:

SECURITY ANSWER:

NOTES:

WEBSITE:

USERNAME:

PASSWORD:

EMAIL USED:

SECURITY ANSWER:

NOTES:

WEBSITE:

USERNAME:

PASSWORD:

EMAIL USED:

SECURITY ANSWER:

NOTES:

PASSWORD ORGANIZER

WEBSITE:

USERNAME:

PASSWORD:

EMAIL USED:

SECURITY ANSWER:

NOTES:

WEBSITE:

USERNAME:

PASSWORD:

EMAIL USED:

SECURITY ANSWER:

NOTES:

WEBSITE:

USERNAME:

PASSWORD:

EMAIL USED:

SECURITY ANSWER:

NOTES:

WEBSITE:

USERNAME:

PASSWORD:

EMAIL USED:

SECURITY ANSWER:

NOTES:

PASSWORD ORGANIZER

WEBSITE:

USERNAME:

PASSWORD:

EMAIL USED:

SECURITY ANSWER:

NOTES:

WEBSITE:

USERNAME:

PASSWORD:

EMAIL USED:

SECURITY ANSWER:

NOTES:

WEBSITE:

USERNAME:

PASSWORD:

EMAIL USED:

SECURITY ANSWER:

NOTES:

WEBSITE:

USERNAME:

PASSWORD:

EMAIL USED:

SECURITY ANSWER:

NOTES:

M

PASSWORD ORGANIZER

WEBSITE:

USERNAME: __________

PASSWORD: __________

EMAIL USED: __________

SECURITY ANSWER: __________

NOTES: __________

WEBSITE:

USERNAME: __________

PASSWORD: __________

EMAIL USED: __________

SECURITY ANSWER: __________

NOTES: __________

WEBSITE:

USERNAME: __________

PASSWORD: __________

EMAIL USED: __________

SECURITY ANSWER: __________

NOTES: __________

WEBSITE:

USERNAME: __________

PASSWORD: __________

EMAIL USED: __________

SECURITY ANSWER: __________

NOTES: __________

PASSWORD ORGANIZER

WEBSITE:

USERNAME:

PASSWORD:

EMAIL USED:

SECURITY ANSWER:

NOTES:

WEBSITE:

USERNAME:

PASSWORD:

EMAIL USED:

SECURITY ANSWER:

NOTES:

WEBSITE:

USERNAME:

PASSWORD:

EMAIL USED:

SECURITY ANSWER:

NOTES:

WEBSITE:

USERNAME:

PASSWORD:

EMAIL USED:

SECURITY ANSWER:

NOTES:

PASSWORD ORGANIZER

WEBSITE:

USERNAME:

PASSWORD:

EMAIL USED:

SECURITY ANSWER:

NOTES:

WEBSITE:

USERNAME:

PASSWORD:

EMAIL USED:

SECURITY ANSWER:

NOTES:

WEBSITE:

USERNAME:

PASSWORD:

EMAIL USED:

SECURITY ANSWER:

NOTES:

WEBSITE:

USERNAME:

PASSWORD:

EMAIL USED:

SECURITY ANSWER:

NOTES:

PASSWORD ORGANIZER

WEBSITE:

USERNAME:

PASSWORD:

EMAIL USED:

SECURITY ANSWER:

NOTES:

WEBSITE:

USERNAME:

PASSWORD:

EMAIL USED:

SECURITY ANSWER:

NOTES:

WEBSITE:

USERNAME:

PASSWORD:

EMAIL USED:

SECURITY ANSWER:

NOTES:

WEBSITE:

USERNAME:

PASSWORD:

EMAIL USED:

SECURITY ANSWER:

NOTES:

N

PASSWORD ORGANIZER

WEBSITE:

USERNAME:

PASSWORD:

EMAIL USED:

SECURITY ANSWER:

NOTES:

WEBSITE:

USERNAME:

PASSWORD:

EMAIL USED:

SECURITY ANSWER:

NOTES:

WEBSITE:

USERNAME:

PASSWORD:

EMAIL USED:

SECURITY ANSWER:

NOTES:

WEBSITE:

USERNAME:

PASSWORD:

EMAIL USED:

SECURITY ANSWER:

NOTES:

PASSWORD ORGANIZER

WEBSITE:

USERNAME: ______

PASSWORD: ______

EMAIL USED: ______

SECURITY ANSWER: ______

NOTES: ______

WEBSITE:

USERNAME: ______

PASSWORD: ______

EMAIL USED: ______

SECURITY ANSWER: ______

NOTES: ______

WEBSITE:

USERNAME: ______

PASSWORD: ______

EMAIL USED: ______

SECURITY ANSWER: ______

NOTES: ______

WEBSITE:

USERNAME: ______

PASSWORD: ______

EMAIL USED: ______

SECURITY ANSWER: ______

NOTES: ______

PASSWORD ORGANIZER

WEBSITE:
USERNAME:
PASSWORD:
EMAIL USED:
SECURITY ANSWER:
NOTES:

WEBSITE:
USERNAME:
PASSWORD:
EMAIL USED:
SECURITY ANSWER:
NOTES:

WEBSITE:
USERNAME:
PASSWORD:
EMAIL USED:
SECURITY ANSWER:
NOTES:

WEBSITE:
USERNAME:
PASSWORD:
EMAIL USED:
SECURITY ANSWER:
NOTES:

PASSWORD ORGANIZER

WEBSITE:

USERNAME:

PASSWORD:

EMAIL USED:

SECURITY ANSWER:

NOTES:

WEBSITE:

USERNAME:

PASSWORD:

EMAIL USED:

SECURITY ANSWER:

NOTES:

WEBSITE:

USERNAME:

PASSWORD:

EMAIL USED:

SECURITY ANSWER:

NOTES:

WEBSITE:

USERNAME:

PASSWORD:

EMAIL USED:

SECURITY ANSWER:

NOTES:

O

PASSWORD ORGANIZER

WEBSITE:

USERNAME: ____________________

PASSWORD: ____________________

EMAIL USED: ____________________

SECURITY ANSWER: ____________________

NOTES: ____________________

WEBSITE:

USERNAME: ____________________

PASSWORD: ____________________

EMAIL USED: ____________________

SECURITY ANSWER: ____________________

NOTES: ____________________

WEBSITE:

USERNAME: ____________________

PASSWORD: ____________________

EMAIL USED: ____________________

SECURITY ANSWER: ____________________

NOTES: ____________________

WEBSITE:

USERNAME: ____________________

PASSWORD: ____________________

EMAIL USED: ____________________

SECURITY ANSWER: ____________________

NOTES: ____________________

PASSWORD ORGANIZER

WEBSITE:

USERNAME:

PASSWORD:

EMAIL USED:

SECURITY ANSWER:

NOTES:

WEBSITE:

USERNAME:

PASSWORD:

EMAIL USED:

SECURITY ANSWER:

NOTES:

WEBSITE:

USERNAME:

PASSWORD:

EMAIL USED:

SECURITY ANSWER:

NOTES:

WEBSITE:

USERNAME:

PASSWORD:

EMAIL USED:

SECURITY ANSWER:

NOTES:

PASSWORD ORGANIZER

WEBSITE:

USERNAME:

PASSWORD:

EMAIL USED:

SECURITY ANSWER:

NOTES:

WEBSITE:

USERNAME:

PASSWORD:

EMAIL USED:

SECURITY ANSWER:

NOTES:

WEBSITE:

USERNAME:

PASSWORD:

EMAIL USED:

SECURITY ANSWER:

NOTES:

WEBSITE:

USERNAME:

PASSWORD:

EMAIL USED:

SECURITY ANSWER:

NOTES:

PASSWORD ORGANIZER

WEBSITE: ______________________

USERNAME: ______________________
PASSWORD: ______________________
EMAIL USED: ______________________
SECURITY ANSWER: ______________________
NOTES: ______________________

WEBSITE: ______________________

USERNAME: ______________________
PASSWORD: ______________________
EMAIL USED: ______________________
SECURITY ANSWER: ______________________
NOTES: ______________________

WEBSITE: ______________________

USERNAME: ______________________
PASSWORD: ______________________
EMAIL USED: ______________________
SECURITY ANSWER: ______________________
NOTES: ______________________

WEBSITE: ______________________

USERNAME: ______________________
PASSWORD: ______________________
EMAIL USED: ______________________
SECURITY ANSWER: ______________________
NOTES: ______________________

P

PASSWORD ORGANIZER

WEBSITE:

USERNAME: ______

PASSWORD: ______

EMAIL USED: ______

SECURITY ANSWER: ______

NOTES: ______

WEBSITE:

USERNAME: ______

PASSWORD: ______

EMAIL USED: ______

SECURITY ANSWER: ______

NOTES: ______

WEBSITE:

USERNAME: ______

PASSWORD: ______

EMAIL USED: ______

SECURITY ANSWER: ______

NOTES: ______

WEBSITE:

USERNAME: ______

PASSWORD: ______

EMAIL USED: ______

SECURITY ANSWER: ______

NOTES: ______

PASSWORD ORGANIZER

WEBSITE:

USERNAME:

PASSWORD:

EMAIL USED:

SECURITY ANSWER:

NOTES:

WEBSITE:

USERNAME:

PASSWORD:

EMAIL USED:

SECURITY ANSWER:

NOTES:

WEBSITE:

USERNAME:

PASSWORD:

EMAIL USED:

SECURITY ANSWER:

NOTES:

WEBSITE:

USERNAME:

PASSWORD:

EMAIL USED:

SECURITY ANSWER:

NOTES:

PASSWORD ORGANIZER

WEBSITE:

USERNAME:

PASSWORD:

EMAIL USED:

SECURITY ANSWER:

NOTES:

WEBSITE:

USERNAME:

PASSWORD:

EMAIL USED:

SECURITY ANSWER:

NOTES:

WEBSITE:

USERNAME:

PASSWORD:

EMAIL USED:

SECURITY ANSWER:

NOTES:

WEBSITE:

USERNAME:

PASSWORD:

EMAIL USED:

SECURITY ANSWER:

NOTES:

PASSWORD ORGANIZER

WEBSITE:

USERNAME:

PASSWORD:

EMAIL USED:

SECURITY ANSWER:

NOTES:

WEBSITE:

USERNAME:

PASSWORD:

EMAIL USED:

SECURITY ANSWER:

NOTES:

WEBSITE:

USERNAME:

PASSWORD:

EMAIL USED:

SECURITY ANSWER:

NOTES:

WEBSITE:

USERNAME:

PASSWORD:

EMAIL USED:

SECURITY ANSWER:

NOTES:

Q

PASSWORD ORGANIZER

WEBSITE:

USERNAME:

PASSWORD:

EMAIL USED:

SECURITY ANSWER:

NOTES:

WEBSITE:

USERNAME:

PASSWORD:

EMAIL USED:

SECURITY ANSWER:

NOTES:

WEBSITE:

USERNAME:

PASSWORD:

EMAIL USED:

SECURITY ANSWER:

NOTES:

WEBSITE:

USERNAME:

PASSWORD:

EMAIL USED:

SECURITY ANSWER:

NOTES:

PASSWORD ORGANIZER

WEBSITE:

USERNAME:

PASSWORD:

EMAIL USED:

SECURITY ANSWER:

NOTES:

WEBSITE:

USERNAME:

PASSWORD:

EMAIL USED:

SECURITY ANSWER:

NOTES:

WEBSITE:

USERNAME:

PASSWORD:

EMAIL USED:

SECURITY ANSWER:

NOTES:

WEBSITE:

USERNAME:

PASSWORD:

EMAIL USED:

SECURITY ANSWER:

NOTES:

PASSWORD ORGANIZER

WEBSITE:

USERNAME:

PASSWORD:

EMAIL USED:

SECURITY ANSWER:

NOTES:

WEBSITE:

USERNAME:

PASSWORD:

EMAIL USED:

SECURITY ANSWER:

NOTES:

WEBSITE:

USERNAME:

PASSWORD:

EMAIL USED:

SECURITY ANSWER:

NOTES:

WEBSITE:

USERNAME:

PASSWORD:

EMAIL USED:

SECURITY ANSWER:

NOTES:

PASSWORD ORGANIZER

WEBSITE:

USERNAME:

PASSWORD:

EMAIL USED:

SECURITY ANSWER:

NOTES:

WEBSITE:

USERNAME:

PASSWORD:

EMAIL USED:

SECURITY ANSWER:

NOTES:

WEBSITE:

USERNAME:

PASSWORD:

EMAIL USED:

SECURITY ANSWER:

NOTES:

WEBSITE:

USERNAME:

PASSWORD:

EMAIL USED:

SECURITY ANSWER:

NOTES:

R

PASSWORD ORGANIZER

WEBSITE:

USERNAME: ______

PASSWORD: ______

EMAIL USED: ______

SECURITY ANSWER: ______

NOTES: ______

WEBSITE:

USERNAME: ______

PASSWORD: ______

EMAIL USED: ______

SECURITY ANSWER: ______

NOTES: ______

WEBSITE:

USERNAME: ______

PASSWORD: ______

EMAIL USED: ______

SECURITY ANSWER: ______

NOTES: ______

WEBSITE:

USERNAME: ______

PASSWORD: ______

EMAIL USED: ______

SECURITY ANSWER: ______

NOTES: ______

PASSWORD ORGANIZER

WEBSITE:

USERNAME:
PASSWORD:
EMAIL USED:
SECURITY ANSWER:
NOTES:

WEBSITE:

USERNAME:
PASSWORD:
EMAIL USED:
SECURITY ANSWER:
NOTES:

WEBSITE:

USERNAME:
PASSWORD:
EMAIL USED:
SECURITY ANSWER:
NOTES:

WEBSITE:

USERNAME:
PASSWORD:
EMAIL USED:
SECURITY ANSWER:
NOTES:

PASSWORD ORGANIZER

WEBSITE:

USERNAME:

PASSWORD:

EMAIL USED:

SECURITY ANSWER:

NOTES:

WEBSITE:

USERNAME:

PASSWORD:

EMAIL USED:

SECURITY ANSWER:

NOTES:

WEBSITE:

USERNAME:

PASSWORD:

EMAIL USED:

SECURITY ANSWER:

NOTES:

WEBSITE:

USERNAME:

PASSWORD:

EMAIL USED:

SECURITY ANSWER:

NOTES:

PASSWORD ORGANIZER

WEBSITE:

USERNAME:

PASSWORD:

EMAIL USED:

SECURITY ANSWER:

NOTES:

WEBSITE:

USERNAME:

PASSWORD:

EMAIL USED:

SECURITY ANSWER:

NOTES:

WEBSITE:

USERNAME:

PASSWORD:

EMAIL USED:

SECURITY ANSWER:

NOTES:

WEBSITE:

USERNAME:

PASSWORD:

EMAIL USED:

SECURITY ANSWER:

NOTES:

S

PASSWORD ORGANIZER

WEBSITE:

USERNAME:

PASSWORD:

EMAIL USED:

SECURITY ANSWER:

NOTES:

WEBSITE:

USERNAME:

PASSWORD:

EMAIL USED:

SECURITY ANSWER:

NOTES:

WEBSITE:

USERNAME:

PASSWORD:

EMAIL USED:

SECURITY ANSWER:

NOTES:

WEBSITE:

USERNAME:

PASSWORD:

EMAIL USED:

SECURITY ANSWER:

NOTES:

PASSWORD ORGANIZER

WEBSITE:

USERNAME: ______________________

PASSWORD: ______________________

EMAIL USED: ______________________

SECURITY ANSWER: ______________________

NOTES: ______________________

WEBSITE:

USERNAME: ______________________

PASSWORD: ______________________

EMAIL USED: ______________________

SECURITY ANSWER: ______________________

NOTES: ______________________

WEBSITE:

USERNAME: ______________________

PASSWORD: ______________________

EMAIL USED: ______________________

SECURITY ANSWER: ______________________

NOTES: ______________________

WEBSITE:

USERNAME: ______________________

PASSWORD: ______________________

EMAIL USED: ______________________

SECURITY ANSWER: ______________________

NOTES: ______________________

PASSWORD ORGANIZER

WEBSITE:

USERNAME:

PASSWORD:

EMAIL USED:

SECURITY ANSWER:

NOTES:

WEBSITE:

USERNAME:

PASSWORD:

EMAIL USED:

SECURITY ANSWER:

NOTES:

WEBSITE:

USERNAME:

PASSWORD:

EMAIL USED:

SECURITY ANSWER:

NOTES:

WEBSITE:

USERNAME:

PASSWORD:

EMAIL USED:

SECURITY ANSWER:

NOTES:

PASSWORD ORGANIZER

WEBSITE:

USERNAME:

PASSWORD:

EMAIL USED:

SECURITY ANSWER:

NOTES:

WEBSITE:

USERNAME:

PASSWORD:

EMAIL USED:

SECURITY ANSWER:

NOTES:

WEBSITE:

USERNAME:

PASSWORD:

EMAIL USED:

SECURITY ANSWER:

NOTES:

WEBSITE:

USERNAME:

PASSWORD:

EMAIL USED:

SECURITY ANSWER:

NOTES:

T

PASSWORD ORGANIZER

WEBSITE:

USERNAME:

PASSWORD:

EMAIL USED:

SECURITY ANSWER:

NOTES:

WEBSITE:

USERNAME:

PASSWORD:

EMAIL USED:

SECURITY ANSWER:

NOTES:

WEBSITE:

USERNAME:

PASSWORD:

EMAIL USED:

SECURITY ANSWER:

NOTES:

WEBSITE:

USERNAME:

PASSWORD:

EMAIL USED:

SECURITY ANSWER:

NOTES:

PASSWORD ORGANIZER

WEBSITE:

USERNAME:

PASSWORD:

EMAIL USED:

SECURITY ANSWER:

NOTES:

WEBSITE:

USERNAME:

PASSWORD:

EMAIL USED:

SECURITY ANSWER:

NOTES:

WEBSITE:

USERNAME:

PASSWORD:

EMAIL USED:

SECURITY ANSWER:

NOTES:

WEBSITE:

USERNAME:

PASSWORD:

EMAIL USED:

SECURITY ANSWER:

NOTES:

PASSWORD ORGANIZER

WEBSITE:

USERNAME:

PASSWORD:

EMAIL USED:

SECURITY ANSWER:

NOTES:

WEBSITE:

USERNAME:

PASSWORD:

EMAIL USED:

SECURITY ANSWER:

NOTES:

WEBSITE:

USERNAME:

PASSWORD:

EMAIL USED:

SECURITY ANSWER:

NOTES:

WEBSITE:

USERNAME:

PASSWORD:

EMAIL USED:

SECURITY ANSWER:

NOTES:

PASSWORD ORGANIZER

WEBSITE:

USERNAME:

PASSWORD:

EMAIL USED:

SECURITY ANSWER:

NOTES:

WEBSITE:

USERNAME:

PASSWORD:

EMAIL USED:

SECURITY ANSWER:

NOTES:

WEBSITE:

USERNAME:

PASSWORD:

EMAIL USED:

SECURITY ANSWER:

NOTES:

WEBSITE:

USERNAME:

PASSWORD:

EMAIL USED:

SECURITY ANSWER:

NOTES:

U

PASSWORD ORGANIZER

WEBSITE:

USERNAME:

PASSWORD:

EMAIL USED:

SECURITY ANSWER:

NOTES:

WEBSITE:

USERNAME:

PASSWORD:

EMAIL USED:

SECURITY ANSWER:

NOTES:

WEBSITE:

USERNAME:

PASSWORD:

EMAIL USED:

SECURITY ANSWER:

NOTES:

WEBSITE:

USERNAME:

PASSWORD:

EMAIL USED:

SECURITY ANSWER:

NOTES:

PASSWORD ORGANIZER

WEBSITE:

USERNAME:

PASSWORD:

EMAIL USED:

SECURITY ANSWER:

NOTES:

WEBSITE:

USERNAME:

PASSWORD:

EMAIL USED:

SECURITY ANSWER:

NOTES:

WEBSITE:

USERNAME:

PASSWORD:

EMAIL USED:

SECURITY ANSWER:

NOTES:

WEBSITE:

USERNAME:

PASSWORD:

EMAIL USED:

SECURITY ANSWER:

NOTES:

PASSWORD ORGANIZER

WEBSITE:

USERNAME:

PASSWORD:

EMAIL USED:

SECURITY ANSWER:

NOTES:

WEBSITE:

USERNAME:

PASSWORD:

EMAIL USED:

SECURITY ANSWER:

NOTES:

WEBSITE:

USERNAME:

PASSWORD:

EMAIL USED:

SECURITY ANSWER:

NOTES:

WEBSITE:

USERNAME:

PASSWORD:

EMAIL USED:

SECURITY ANSWER:

NOTES:

PASSWORD ORGANIZER

WEBSITE:

USERNAME:

PASSWORD:

EMAIL USED:

SECURITY ANSWER:

NOTES:

WEBSITE:

USERNAME:

PASSWORD:

EMAIL USED:

SECURITY ANSWER:

NOTES:

WEBSITE:

USERNAME:

PASSWORD:

EMAIL USED:

SECURITY ANSWER:

NOTES:

WEBSITE:

USERNAME:

PASSWORD:

EMAIL USED:

SECURITY ANSWER:

NOTES:

V

PASSWORD ORGANIZER

WEBSITE:
USERNAME:
PASSWORD:
EMAIL USED:
SECURITY ANSWER:
NOTES:

WEBSITE:
USERNAME:
PASSWORD:
EMAIL USED:
SECURITY ANSWER:
NOTES:

WEBSITE:
USERNAME:
PASSWORD:
EMAIL USED:
SECURITY ANSWER:
NOTES:

WEBSITE:
USERNAME:
PASSWORD:
EMAIL USED:
SECURITY ANSWER:
NOTES:

PASSWORD ORGANIZER

WEBSITE:

USERNAME:

PASSWORD:

EMAIL USED:

SECURITY ANSWER:

NOTES:

WEBSITE:

USERNAME:

PASSWORD:

EMAIL USED:

SECURITY ANSWER:

NOTES:

WEBSITE:

USERNAME:

PASSWORD:

EMAIL USED:

SECURITY ANSWER:

NOTES:

WEBSITE:

USERNAME:

PASSWORD:

EMAIL USED:

SECURITY ANSWER:

NOTES:

PASSWORD ORGANIZER

WEBSITE:

USERNAME:

PASSWORD:

EMAIL USED:

SECURITY ANSWER:

NOTES:

WEBSITE:

USERNAME:

PASSWORD:

EMAIL USED:

SECURITY ANSWER:

NOTES:

WEBSITE:

USERNAME:

PASSWORD:

EMAIL USED:

SECURITY ANSWER:

NOTES:

WEBSITE:

USERNAME:

PASSWORD:

EMAIL USED:

SECURITY ANSWER:

NOTES:

PASSWORD ORGANIZER

WEBSITE:

USERNAME:

PASSWORD:

EMAIL USED:

SECURITY ANSWER:

NOTES:

WEBSITE:

USERNAME:

PASSWORD:

EMAIL USED:

SECURITY ANSWER:

NOTES:

WEBSITE:

USERNAME:

PASSWORD:

EMAIL USED:

SECURITY ANSWER:

NOTES:

WEBSITE:

USERNAME:

PASSWORD:

EMAIL USED:

SECURITY ANSWER:

NOTES:

W

PASSWORD ORGANIZER

WEBSITE:

USERNAME:

PASSWORD:

EMAIL USED:

SECURITY ANSWER:

NOTES:

WEBSITE:

USERNAME:

PASSWORD:

EMAIL USED:

SECURITY ANSWER:

NOTES:

WEBSITE:

USERNAME:

PASSWORD:

EMAIL USED:

SECURITY ANSWER:

NOTES:

WEBSITE:

USERNAME:

PASSWORD:

EMAIL USED:

SECURITY ANSWER:

NOTES:

PASSWORD ORGANIZER

WEBSITE:

USERNAME:

PASSWORD:

EMAIL USED:

SECURITY ANSWER:

NOTES:

WEBSITE:

USERNAME:

PASSWORD:

EMAIL USED:

SECURITY ANSWER:

NOTES:

WEBSITE:

USERNAME:

PASSWORD:

EMAIL USED:

SECURITY ANSWER:

NOTES:

WEBSITE:

USERNAME:

PASSWORD:

EMAIL USED:

SECURITY ANSWER:

NOTES:

PASSWORD ORGANIZER

WEBSITE:

USERNAME:

PASSWORD:

EMAIL USED:

SECURITY ANSWER:

NOTES:

WEBSITE:

USERNAME:

PASSWORD:

EMAIL USED:

SECURITY ANSWER:

NOTES:

WEBSITE:

USERNAME:

PASSWORD:

EMAIL USED:

SECURITY ANSWER:

NOTES:

WEBSITE:

USERNAME:

PASSWORD:

EMAIL USED:

SECURITY ANSWER:

NOTES:

PASSWORD ORGANIZER

WEBSITE:

USERNAME:

PASSWORD:

EMAIL USED:

SECURITY ANSWER:

NOTES:

WEBSITE:

USERNAME:

PASSWORD:

EMAIL USED:

SECURITY ANSWER:

NOTES:

WEBSITE:

USERNAME:

PASSWORD:

EMAIL USED:

SECURITY ANSWER:

NOTES:

WEBSITE:

USERNAME:

PASSWORD:

EMAIL USED:

SECURITY ANSWER:

NOTES:

X

PASSWORD ORGANIZER

WEBSITE:

USERNAME:

PASSWORD:

EMAIL USED:

SECURITY ANSWER:

NOTES:

WEBSITE:

USERNAME:

PASSWORD:

EMAIL USED:

SECURITY ANSWER:

NOTES:

WEBSITE:

USERNAME:

PASSWORD:

EMAIL USED:

SECURITY ANSWER:

NOTES:

WEBSITE:

USERNAME:

PASSWORD:

EMAIL USED:

SECURITY ANSWER:

NOTES:

PASSWORD ORGANIZER

WEBSITE:

USERNAME: ____________________

PASSWORD: ____________________

EMAIL USED: ____________________

SECURITY ANSWER: ____________________

NOTES: ____________________

WEBSITE:

USERNAME: ____________________

PASSWORD: ____________________

EMAIL USED: ____________________

SECURITY ANSWER: ____________________

NOTES: ____________________

WEBSITE:

USERNAME: ____________________

PASSWORD: ____________________

EMAIL USED: ____________________

SECURITY ANSWER: ____________________

NOTES: ____________________

WEBSITE:

USERNAME: ____________________

PASSWORD: ____________________

EMAIL USED: ____________________

SECURITY ANSWER: ____________________

NOTES: ____________________

PASSWORD ORGANIZER

WEBSITE:

USERNAME:

PASSWORD:

EMAIL USED:

SECURITY ANSWER:

NOTES:

WEBSITE:

USERNAME:

PASSWORD:

EMAIL USED:

SECURITY ANSWER:

NOTES:

WEBSITE:

USERNAME:

PASSWORD:

EMAIL USED:

SECURITY ANSWER:

NOTES:

WEBSITE:

USERNAME:

PASSWORD:

EMAIL USED:

SECURITY ANSWER:

NOTES:

PASSWORD ORGANIZER

WEBSITE:

USERNAME:

PASSWORD:

EMAIL USED:

SECURITY ANSWER:

NOTES:

WEBSITE:

USERNAME:

PASSWORD:

EMAIL USED:

SECURITY ANSWER:

NOTES:

WEBSITE:

USERNAME:

PASSWORD:

EMAIL USED:

SECURITY ANSWER:

NOTES:

WEBSITE:

USERNAME:

PASSWORD:

EMAIL USED:

SECURITY ANSWER:

NOTES:

Y

PASSWORD ORGANIZER

WEBSITE:

USERNAME:

PASSWORD:

EMAIL USED:

SECURITY ANSWER:

NOTES:

WEBSITE:

USERNAME:

PASSWORD:

EMAIL USED:

SECURITY ANSWER:

NOTES:

WEBSITE:

USERNAME:

PASSWORD:

EMAIL USED:

SECURITY ANSWER:

NOTES:

WEBSITE:

USERNAME:

PASSWORD:

EMAIL USED:

SECURITY ANSWER:

NOTES:

PASSWORD ORGANIZER

WEBSITE:

USERNAME:

PASSWORD:

EMAIL USED:

SECURITY ANSWER:

NOTES:

WEBSITE:

USERNAME:

PASSWORD:

EMAIL USED:

SECURITY ANSWER:

NOTES:

WEBSITE:

USERNAME:

PASSWORD:

EMAIL USED:

SECURITY ANSWER:

NOTES:

WEBSITE:

USERNAME:

PASSWORD:

EMAIL USED:

SECURITY ANSWER:

NOTES:

PASSWORD ORGANIZER

WEBSITE:

USERNAME:

PASSWORD:

EMAIL USED:

SECURITY ANSWER:

NOTES:

WEBSITE:

USERNAME:

PASSWORD:

EMAIL USED:

SECURITY ANSWER:

NOTES:

WEBSITE:

USERNAME:

PASSWORD:

EMAIL USED:

SECURITY ANSWER:

NOTES:

WEBSITE:

USERNAME:

PASSWORD:

EMAIL USED:

SECURITY ANSWER:

NOTES:

PASSWORD ORGANIZER

WEBSITE:

USERNAME:

PASSWORD:

EMAIL USED:

SECURITY ANSWER:

NOTES:

WEBSITE:

USERNAME:

PASSWORD:

EMAIL USED:

SECURITY ANSWER:

NOTES:

WEBSITE:

USERNAME:

PASSWORD:

EMAIL USED:

SECURITY ANSWER:

NOTES:

WEBSITE:

USERNAME:

PASSWORD:

EMAIL USED:

SECURITY ANSWER:

NOTES:

Z

PASSWORD ORGANIZER

WEBSITE:

USERNAME:

PASSWORD:

EMAIL USED:

SECURITY ANSWER:

NOTES:

WEBSITE:

USERNAME:

PASSWORD:

EMAIL USED:

SECURITY ANSWER:

NOTES:

WEBSITE:

USERNAME:

PASSWORD:

EMAIL USED:

SECURITY ANSWER:

NOTES:

WEBSITE:

USERNAME:

PASSWORD:

EMAIL USED:

SECURITY ANSWER:

NOTES:

PASSWORD ORGANIZER

WEBSITE:

USERNAME:

PASSWORD:

EMAIL USED:

SECURITY ANSWER:

NOTES:

WEBSITE:

USERNAME:

PASSWORD:

EMAIL USED:

SECURITY ANSWER:

NOTES:

WEBSITE:

USERNAME:

PASSWORD:

EMAIL USED:

SECURITY ANSWER:

NOTES:

WEBSITE:

USERNAME:

PASSWORD:

EMAIL USED:

SECURITY ANSWER:

NOTES:

PASSWORD ORGANIZER

WEBSITE:

USERNAME: ______

PASSWORD: ______

EMAIL USED: ______

SECURITY ANSWER: ______

NOTES: ______

WEBSITE:

USERNAME: ______

PASSWORD: ______

EMAIL USED: ______

SECURITY ANSWER: ______

NOTES: ______

WEBSITE:

USERNAME: ______

PASSWORD: ______

EMAIL USED: ______

SECURITY ANSWER: ______

NOTES: ______

WEBSITE:

USERNAME: ______

PASSWORD: ______

EMAIL USED: ______

SECURITY ANSWER: ______

NOTES: ______

PASSWORD ORGANIZER

WEBSITE:

USERNAME:

PASSWORD:

EMAIL USED:

SECURITY ANSWER:

NOTES:

WEBSITE:

USERNAME:

PASSWORD:

EMAIL USED:

SECURITY ANSWER:

NOTES:

WEBSITE:

USERNAME:

PASSWORD:

EMAIL USED:

SECURITY ANSWER:

NOTES:

WEBSITE:

USERNAME:

PASSWORD:

EMAIL USED:

SECURITY ANSWER:

NOTES:

PASSWORD ORGANIZER

WEBSITE:

USERNAME:

PASSWORD:

EMAIL USED:

SECURITY ANSWER:

NOTES:

WEBSITE:

USERNAME:

PASSWORD:

EMAIL USED:

SECURITY ANSWER:

NOTES:

WEBSITE:

USERNAME:

PASSWORD:

EMAIL USED:

SECURITY ANSWER:

NOTES:

WEBSITE:

USERNAME:

PASSWORD:

EMAIL USED:

SECURITY ANSWER:

NOTES:

www.ingramcontent.com/pod-product-compliance
Lightning Source LLC
LaVergne TN
LVHW022227200926
848481LV00006B/2154